THE OFFICIAL
OHIOANS' GUIDE
TO
MICHIGAN JOKES

THE OFFICIAL

OHIOANS' GUIDE

TO

MICHIGAN JOKES

by

Richard Loren Rahn

SHENANDOAH PRESS   BLOOMFIELD HILLS, MICHIGAN

Published by
Shenandoah Press
P.O. Box 1090
Bloomfield Hills, Michigan 48303

ISBN 0-9613311-1-9

Printed in U.S.A.

CONTENTS

FOREWORD

The rivalry between Ohio State University and the University of Michigan is one of the oldest and most celebrated in the country, but the rivalry goes beyond just the colleges. No one knows this better than I.

Growing up in Michigan, I attended many U of M games and became a true-blue Michigan fan. But times change and my father moved to Ohio, and I found myself attending OSU. Now half my family lives in Ohio, the other half in Michigan. When we all get together, more than a few barbs between the states are exchanged.

Wanting to pursue this rivalry further, I took out ads in several Michigan newspapers asking for Ohio/OSU jokes, meaning to do the same in Ohio—requesting Michigan jokes. I never got the chance! The response was overwhelming! Now only did I receive hundreds of jokes and letters, but also a lot of media attention. The story was picked up by some radio stations in Cleveland who gave out my address daily, and urged its listeners to send me Michigan jokes in retaliation! Soon I was getting more mail from Ohio than Michigan.

This book is a collection of some of the more printable jokes I received. I hope you enjoy them.

—Richard L. Rahn

Heard any good Michigan jokes lately?
If so, send 'em in!

P.O. Box 1090
Bloomfield Hills, MI 48303

(I know, I know, it's in Michigan!)

ACKNOWLEDGMENTS

I would really like to thank everyone in the "Buckeye State" for the hundreds of jokes and letters I received.

I want to thank Brian for his great drawings, and my mom and dad for their dollar support. Also—Amy and Zeno, Bucks and Sunk, four famous Ohioans. Plus "The Bearded Man."

THE OFFICIAL
OHIOANS' GUIDE
TO
MICHIGAN JOKES

MICHIGAN INTELLECT

Most of Michigan is so slow, it takes them an hour and a half to watch 60 minutes!!

☆ ☆ ☆

What are the three most difficult years in a Michigander's life?

Second grade!

☆ ☆ ☆

Why do Michiganders make the best secret agents?

Even under torture they can't remember what they have been assigned to do!!

What do you call a twenty-eight year old Michigander in the fifth grade?

A prodigy!

How many Michiganders does it take to wash a car?

Two. One to hold the sponge, and one to drive the car back and forth!!

What do Michiganders have printed on the soles of their shoes?

This Side Down!

Do you know why Michiganders don't make kool-aid?

They have trouble getting two quarts of water into that little package!

What is the shortest book in the world?

Michigan 'Wit and Wisdom.'

Michiganders don't eat M&Ms. They get tired of trying to peel them!!

They have just announced for the first time in history a new medical development in Michigan. They performed the first transplant of the human appendix!

Did you hear about the Michigan jigsaw puzzle?

It only has one piece!

Did you hear about the Michigander who turned down a blowjob because he thought it would interfere with his unemployment benefits!

During the last Ohio/Michigan war do you know how the Ohioans took over Michigan?

The Ohio army marched across the Michigan border backwards and the Michiganders thought they were leaving!

MICHIGAN BANK: You bring in a toaster and they give you $500.00!

How many Michiganders does it take to pull off a kidnapping?

Six. One to kidnap the victim, and five to write the ransom note!

☆ ☆ ☆

Why can't Michiganders eat pickles!

They can't get their heads into the jar!

☆ ☆ ☆

What does it say at the top of a Michigander's ladder?

STOP!

☆ ☆ ☆

Why are there no ice cubes in Michigan?

They lost the recipe!

Why are there no skydivers from Michigan?

What good is a parachute if you can't count to ten!

Did you hear what happened to the Detroit library?

Someone stole the book!

The Michigan couple adopted a three-month-old war orphan and decided to learn Vietnamese so they'd understand what the baby was saying when it grew up!!

What happened when the Michigan terrorist tried to blow up a bus?

He burned his lips on the exhaust pipe!

What do you call a stork that delivers Michigan babies?

A dope peddler!

☆ ☆ ☆

What do you call a Michigander with half a brain?

Gifted!

☆ ☆ ☆

It was the first day on the job for the Michigan plumber. The phone rang and the caller said, "I got a leak in my bathtub." "Go 'head," said the Michigander. "It won't hurt nothin'."

☆ ☆ ☆

Did you hear about the Michigan car pool?

They all meet at work!

If ignorance was bliss, Michigan would be jumping for joy!

Why don't Michigan workers get lunch breaks?
It would take too long to retrain them!

What has an I.Q. of 7?
Eight Michiganders!

Why wasn't Christ born in Michigan?
They couldn't find three wise men and a virgin!!

Do you know why you won't find many full salt shakers in Michigan?

Because it's very hard for them to get the salt through those tiny little holes?

Did you hear about the Michigan man who sued his brains for nonsupport!

What is an awkward animal with a trunk?

A Michigander on vacation!

When visiting Michigan, if a robber threatens to blow your brains out if you don't give him your money—don't give him the money. In Michigan you can live without brains but you can't live without money!

How does the average Michigander spell farm?

E I E I O

What is the definition of an intellectual in Michigan?

A person that doesn't move his lips when he reads!

WOMEN OF MICHIGAN

Why do Michigan women wear high-heeled shoes?

To keep their knuckles from dragging on the ground.

What is the difference between a parrot and a Michigan girl?

You can teach the parrot to say no!

Who won the Michigan beauty pageant?

Nobody!

The Michigan housewife called up the fire department and shouted, "There's a fire! There's a fire!"

"How do we get there?" asked the fireman.

"What happened to your big red truck?"

How did the Michigan girl know she was pregnant?

The hippo died!

What's dumb, ugly and rings your doorbell all the time?

A Michigan Avon lady!!

Did you hear about the Michigan housewife who takes an hour to cook minute rice!

Why can't Michigan women use vibrators?

They keep chipping their teeth!

What is the difference between a urinal and a Michigan girl?

The urinal doesn't follow you around after you use it!

How do Michigan women protect themselves from peeping toms?

They keep the shades up!

Miss Michigan received a very strong recommendation from the judges at the Miss America contest this year. They recommended she go home and stay there!

What is the difference between a Michigan girl and Bigfoot?

One is 750 lbs., is covered with matted hair and smells awful, and the other has big feet!!

What's the difference between a Michigan grand-mother and an elephant?

About seven pounds!

How does a Michigan mother put on her child's underwear?

Yellow in front, brown in back!

Why don't Michigan women breast feed their babies?

It hurts too much to boil their nipples!!

How do you get a Michigan woman to burn her face?

Telephone her while she's ironing!

The Michigan woman had only been married three days when she walked into a drugstore and asked for a bottle of men's deodorant. "The ball type?" asked the clerk. "No," she said, "for his underarms!"

What do you call a great-looking girl in Michigan?

A tourist!!

Two Michigan girls shared a room on the University of Michigan campus. One day the one girl came in and said, "I hear there's a new case of gonorrhea in the dorm." "Good!" said the other one, "I was getting awfully tired of Fresca!"

Why did God invent booze?

So that Michigan girls would have a chance to get laid, too!

What's the difference between garbage and Michigan girls?

Sometimes the garbage gets picked up!

MEN OF MICHIGAN

How many Michiganders does it take to eat possum?

Three. One to eat the possum, and two to watch for cars!!

Did you hear about the Michigander who was up all night studying for his urine test!

What is the most difficult decision a Michigander has to make when he is invited to a formal party?

Whether to wear his red socks or his green socks!

What do you call three Michigan men sitting on the lawn?

Fertilizer!

How do you break a Michigander's finger?

Hit him in the nose!

Two Detroiters went hunting up in the Upper Peninsula. They took along two guns and three dogs. Half an hour later, they came back for more dogs!

☆ ☆ ☆

Did you hear about the Michigan man who had just learned to count to twenty-one when he was arrested for indecent exposure!

How do we know Batman came from Michigan?

Who else would put his jockey shorts over his leotards?

Why is the average age of a soldier in Michigan 50?

They get them right out of high school!

Then there was the Michigan man who took his new tie back to the store because it was too tight for him!!

What do you call a Michigander with a degree?

A liar!

☆ ☆ ☆

Two Michigan men were walking along Lake Huron when suddenly a seagull flying overhead dropped a load right in the one man's eye. "I'll go get some toilet paper," his friend offered. "Don't bother," said the man. "He's probably miles away by now."

Why did they outlaw lynching in Michigan?

The guy who knew how to tie the knots moved!

What is the first thing a Michigander does when he gets out of the shower?

He takes his clothes off!

What do you call a Michigander who is respected, has brains, is well groomed, has money and is an all around gentleman?

A mutation.

"The laundry made a mistake," the Michigan man said to his wife. "This shirt collar is so tight I can hardly breathe. This can't be my shirt."

"It's your shirt all right," said his wife. "You just have your head through the buttonhole!"

What is a proctologist in Michigan called?

A brain surgeon!

How do you stop a Michigander from drowning?

Take your foot off his head.

What is the definition of mass confusion?

Father's Day in Detroit!!

What do Michigan women find attractive about Michigan men!

Their lobotomy scar!!

How do you get a one armed Michigander out of a tree?

Wave to him!

Who has a beard,
wears a dirty white robe and rides a pig?

Laurence of Michigan.

SPORTS IN MICHIGAN

It was the big Ohio State/Michigan game in Columbus. Every seat in the 'horseshoe' was filled—except one. The man sitting beside the empty seat was questioned about it by the man behind him. He proceeded to tell him that he and his wife had been coming here for years, but that his wife had passed on. The man behind him said that he was very sorry, but seeing as how this was the toughest ticket in town to get, couldn't the man have brought someone else along to enjoy the game with him? A friend, or maybe a relative? "I would have," said the man, "but they're all at her funeral."

☆ ☆ ☆

What brings tears to a Michigan mother's eyes?

When she buys her son his first athletic supporter!

Did you hear what happened to the Michigan hockey team?

They drowned during spring training!

What do you call a good looking guy in Ann Arbor?

An Ohio State football player up for a game!

Did you hear what happened to the Michigan water polo team?

Their horses drowned!

What do a football player and a Michigan girl have in common?

Pigskin!!

Why is there artificial turf in Michigan stadium?

To keep the cheerleaders from grazing!

Did you hear about the Indy driver from Michigan who made 23 pit stops?

3 for fuel, 4 to change tires, and 16 to ask directions!

And how about the Michigander who got a pair of water skis for his birthday?

He went insane looking for a hill on Lake Michigan!

Why are the mothers of Michiganders so strong?

From raising dumbbells!

At the first football game of the year in Michigan, the cheerleader looked up at the packed stands and shouted:

"Give me an F!"

"F!" shouted the crowd.

"Give me an I!" she yelled.

"I!" yelled the crowd.

"Give me a G!"

"G!" cried the crowd.

"Give me an H!"

"H!" screamed the crowd.

"Give me a T!"

"T!" screeched the crowd.

"WHAT'S THAT SPELL?"

Complete silence.

Did you hear about the Michigan football star who was dropped from the team for breaking training?

The coach caught him studying!

When the young man applied for the lifeguarding job on Lake Erie, the personnel director asked the boy if he knew how to save a Michigander from drowning. The boy said that he didn't. The director hired him on the spot!

Disgusted with his players during practice, the Michigan coach called the team together and laid down the law. "Look men, before we can make any further progress, we must go back to the fundamentals." He reached over and picked up a ball. "Now this," he said, "is a football. It. . . ."

At this point a Michigan lineman interrupted: "Please coach, not so fast!"

There have been Michigan quarterbacks so dumb that when they won their letter, they had to ask someone to read it to them!

The freshman farm boy showed up at the spring try-outs for the U of M football team. When asked by the coach what position he wanted to play, he said quarterback. The coach handed him the football and said, "Do you think you can pass this?"

"Hell," the boy said, "If I can swallow it, I can pass it!"

What do football players and Michigan girls have in common?

They both shower after the fourth period!

SEX IN MICHIGAN

How do Michiganders reproduce?

They exchange underwear!

What do you get when you cross a gorilla with a Michigander?

A retarded gorilla!

The Michigan girl came home one day in tears and cried, "Daddy, I'm pregnant!"

Her father answered, "Are you sure it's yours?"

What did the Michigander do with his first fifty cent piece?

He married her.

Why don't doctors circumcise Michiganders anymore?
They discovered they were throwing away the best part!

What is foreplay in Michigan?
Cutting eyeholes in your wife's paper bag!

Where can you buy panties made out of fertilizer bags and bras made out of beer cans?

Fredericks of Hamtramck!

Michigan marriage proposal: You're gonna have a what?!

A young man was extolling the virtues of his beautiful bride-to-be. One of his closest friends exclaimed, "You can't be serious about marrying Lisa! Why, she's been to bed with every man in Lansing!"

The young man thought awhile and then said, "Lansing isn't such a big town."

The two Michigan couples got together every Saturday night for years, and boredom had set in. One night after several drinks, they decided to switch partners. The next morning Harold woke up and said to his companion, "Did you enjoy that?"

"I had a terrific time, let's go see how the girls did!"

The bank in the Detroit suburbs had just opened. The young Michigan woman walked in carrying a shopping bag filled with nickels, dimes and quarters. "Did you hoard all this money by yourself?" asked the teller.

"No," said the woman, "my sister whored half of it!"

Did you hear about the Michigan abortion clinic?

There's a one year waiting list!

Two Michigan men were driving home from work. "Let's stop and get a beer at this great new place I found," said the one. "The barstools are numbered and if your number is called, you can go upstairs and have free sex!"

"No kidding," said the other, "Did you ever win?"

"No," said the first one, "But last week my wife won twice!"

What do you call grave robbing in Michigan?

Date night!

A Michigan man was arrested for rape and put into a police lineup. When the victim was ushered in to identify her assailant, the man pointed to her and shouted, "That's her, that's her!"

Michigan man: Can't we keep our marriage a secret?

Michigan woman: But what if we have a baby?

Michigan man: Oh, we'll tell the baby of course.

Why do Michigan men make such lousy lovers?

They always wait until the swelling goes down!

Michigan girl: Can you give me change for this 50 dollar bill?

Bank teller: This isn't a 50 dollar bill, it's a coupon.

Michigan girl: My God, I've been raped!!

What do you get when you cross a Michigander with a monkey?

Nothing. A monkey is too smart to screw a Michigander!!

What do you call a Michigander who practices birth control?

A humanitarian!!

MISCELLANEOUS

Why is the wheelbarrow the greatest of all human inventions?

It taught the Michiganders to walk on their hind legs!!

Why do flies have wings?

So they can beat the Michiganders to the dump!

What is the capital of Michigan?

About forty cents!

What is the best thing to come out of Michigan?

I-75.

☆ ☆ ☆

Did you know in Poland they tell Michigan jokes!

☆ ☆ ☆

What do you call the index finger on a Michigander's hand?

A handkerchief!

☆ ☆ ☆

What is the toughest job in Detroit?

Riding shotgun on the garbage truck!

Did you hear about the Michigander who bought a pet rock?

The next day it ran away!!

The other day two seagulls were spotted flying up-side down over Michigan. Upside-down because they couldn't find anything worth pooping on!!

Why did the aquarium in Ann Arbor close?

The clam died!

What is a set of Michigan stemware?

Three empty grape jelly glasses!

Some Michigan babies are so ugly . . .

The doctors feed them with slingshots!

There was this carload of Michiganders riding through the beautiful farmlands of Ohio, when suddenly they crashed. Now there just happened to be an Ohio farmer out plowing his field, so he rushed over and tried to figure out what to do with them. After some debate, he decided to bury them. When he got through he began to wonder if he had done the right thing, so he called the Highway Patrol. Well, they sent an officer out who assured the farmer he had done the right thing. He asked the farmer if he was sure they were all dead, and the farmer said, "Some of 'em said they weren't, but you know how them Michiganders lie."

What do you call 500 Michiganders at the beach?
Bay of Pigs.

What's a Michigander's idea of a day in the country?
Sitting in the back yard!

How was streaking invented?
They tried to give a Michigander a bath!

What do you call bad breath in Michigan?
Keeping up with the Joneses!

Why don't they have fly swatters in Michigan?
It's against the law to kill the state bird!

What magazine is banned in Michigan?
Good Housekeeping!

What do Michigan and Kinney's have in common?

Lots of loafers!

Why do Michiganders have such pretty noses?

Because they're hand picked!

Two words you never want a Michigander to say to you?

"Hi, neighbor."

What are the first three words a Michigan baby learns?

Attention K-mart shoppers!

Whoever said, "Love thy neighbor," didn't live next to Michigan!

Did you hear about the Michigander who wanted to write "Happy Birthday" on a cake?

For three hours he tried to get that cake into a type-writer!

Why can't Michiganders lie on the beach?

Cats will bury them!

Crying shame: A busload of Michiganders going over a cliff with two empty seats!

How do you make a Michigan hot tub?

Two alka-seltzer in the toilet!

What is a big night in Kalamazoo?

Watching the overloaded machines break down at the laundromat!

Why are Michiganders forbidden to swim in the Ohio lakes?

They leave a ring!

What do you call a pimple on a Michigander's butt?

A brain tumor!

FUN FACTS AND USELESS KNOWLEDGE

ONLY IN MICHIGAN DEPARTMENT

☆   ☆   ☆

Only in Michigan could they have an outbreak of dogs shooting their masters!

In less than a one year period in Michigan, three separate incidents of dogs shooting their masters were reported and documented. The dogs were using everything from .22 pistols to double-barreled, twelve-gauge shotguns!! This is TRUE!

(If this catches on with Ohio canines, we're all in big trouble!)

FAMOUS ONE-TIME
RESIDENTS OF OHIO

J. D. Rockefeller
Doris Day
William H. Taft
Bob Hope
Ulysses S. Grant
Paul Lynde
SIX Miss Americas
William H. McKinley
Jayne Kennedy

Benjamin Harrison
Dean Martin
James Garfield
Dom Deluise
Rutherford B. Hayes
Clark Gable
Warren Harding
Paul Newman

☆ ☆ ☆

FAMOUS PERMANENT
RESIDENTS OF MICHIGAN

Jimmy Hoffa

MICHIGAN HALL OF FAME

MICHIGAN TROUBLE

Ohio and Michigan have been going at it a long time. In 1835 they almost had a full scale war with each other. It seems there was a 400 square mile question about the boundary line between the two.

One thing led to another and pretty soon the Ohio militia (led by Gov. Robert Lucas) were squaring off with Michigan territorial soldiers (led by 21-year-old acting Gov. Stevens T. Mason) across the Maumee River. President Jackson sent peacemakers to the scene and warfare was delayed, although there were several border incidents. (Probably the Michigan troops were throwing sticks of dynamite across the river, and the Ohio militia men were lighting them and throwing them back.) Anyway, Jackson handed down a decision in favor of Ohio (Ohio had much more political clout than the Michigan territories), and Michigan was compensated with the whole western half of the Upper Peninsula and immediate statehood.

Once again, warfare was avoided, but almost 150 years later the battle between these two states rages on. . . .

BUMPER STICKERS
SEEN IN OHIO

Sent in by Paul Svigel, #1 Buckeye football fanatic.

MUCK FICHIGAN

SCREW THE BLUE

MICHIGAN: THE PART OF OHIO NOBODY WANTED.

PANSIES ARE MAIZE AND BLUE, TOO.

☆ ☆ ☆

THE BEST PART OF MICHIGAN IS UNDER WATER.

☆ ☆ ☆

WARNING: I BRAKE FOR ALL ANIMALS EXCEPT WOLVERINES.

☆ ☆ ☆

DIRECTIONS TO ANN ARBOR: NORTH "TILL YOU SMELL IT," WEST "TILL YOU STEP IN IT."

M GO BLOW

☆ ☆ ☆

THEY CALL IT MAIZE, WE CALL IT CORN.

☆ ☆ ☆

BO IS NOT A PERFECT '10'

Others:

☆ ☆ ☆

ANN ARBOR—What gas station is that near?

☆ ☆ ☆

BURY A BUCKEYE—IT WILL GROW
BURY A WOLVERINE—IT WILL ROT

☆ ☆ ☆

Let's give Michigan back to the Fichigan.

MICHIGAN
HEALTH WARNING

If you feel pressure on your head, your eyes are almost pressed shut, and you smell an unusual odor and one foot is cold . . .

you have your sock over your head!